Success Unshackled

LAURA MITCHELL

ABOUT THE AUTHOR

Laura Mitchell, also known as Mrs. Laura, is the founder of the Elite Five-Star organization Daddy Mom Daycare— Child Care Center and Community Center in Denver, Colorado. Assisting families in raising over 5,000 children by providing quality child care within a community center offering employment, funding and resources to families of all walks of life.

Laura Mitchell is a Professional Counselor in her private practice specializing in Relationship and Family Therapy, Group Therapy and Private Counseling. Laura is an international speaker for women's organizations, Department of Corrections, Corporate Training Programs and Prison Ministry.

Her mission is to get women to a place of feeling amazing, successful, accomplished and happy which allows them to embrace all the power they hold within.

www.iamlauramitchell.com

www.URthekey.com

DEDICATION

This book is dedicated to my children Jon
& Ashley, Jeremy & Vandrea, and Jenay & Oscar. You are the
light of my life. You inspired me to share my story, you are
my soldiers through my battles and you keep me humble.
You are my success story. ~ Mom

To my grandchildren—so you may know my journey and
your strength ~ Nana

To my best friend and husband Willie,
I dreamt of a man who was honorable, loving, and kind. A
man that would love me unconditionally and accept me with
all my favor and all my faults. Dreams do come true. ~ Wife

To my parents Larry & Marie,
I would not be the person I am today. Thank you for never
giving up on me. I love you.
~ Laura

TESTIMONIALS for Success Unshackled

"Laura has always been an inspiration and strong voice for those who have found themselves in a place of no hope. She attracts people everywhere she goes because of her positive energy and ability to reach down deep and not only see but draw out the best in them. Her presence and words are infectious, and anyone who has been blessed enough to know her can attest to the power of her influence. Laura has overcome the most detrimental of circumstances; and she's done so with grace and class, and without losing an ounce of her integrity. She's a role model and heroine in the eyes of many women. We always knew she was destined for greatness, but she far exceeded that years ago. Now she's conquering the universe!"

Adrienne Hernandez
Colleague, Engineer and Board of Directors Chair DMD
Denver, Colorado

"I've witnessed complete strangers open up to Laura as if she were their best friend. I've witnessed Laura respond with love and compassion as if they were her best friend. She's something special."

Debra Holt, Psychologist
Newark, New Jersey

"Laura will inspire and bless many lives with her authenticity and courage.

Van Brown
Actor, Motivational Speaker and
Author of Experience the True Nature of Love
Los Angeles, California

"Laura has helped a lot of people become who they are; great leaders and great role models, all because they had someone like her to look up too."

Michael Justin Montoya
Music & Art Collector, Denver, Colorado

"Laura Mitchell's approach to creating a 'Success Unshackled' reality will inspire you to live a limitless life of power and freedom. This great book is a proven guide to help you break free from the various circumstantial and mental chains that hold us back from becoming our greatest selves!"

~~ Dr. Ona Brown ~ The Message Midwife/Speaker Coach/Brand Builder

ACKNOWLEDGMENTS

I acknowledge that I would be nothing if it were not for my Lord and Savior, Jesus Christ. When life was at its lowest, He was by my side. When life is at its heights, He is by my side. I acknowledge Your presence during the writing of this book.

I acknowledge some of the great leaders I have had the pleasure of learning from; Jon Blizz, my life coach, for throwing a match at me and lighting the fire to open up about my past. Dr. Leslie Reo, Donna Hilliard, Dane Hendricks, Barbra Russell, Sonya Utz, Angela Baeza, Dr. Ona Brown, Vishal Morjaria, and Dr. Cheryl George; your mentorship has been priceless.

I acknowledge my Daddy Mom family, those who have crossed the threshold into my life. There are so many of you who have loved and supported me and my family. Thank you.

I acknowledge the many men and women who have or currently serve in the United States Army. Thank you for your commitment. I acknowledge my Army family who proudly and silently serve beside their spouse. You have inspired me to step out of my comfort zone, to drink more coffee, and to know a community of love, laughter, and bravery that I would have never known existed outside the gates. Thank you for your kindness and acceptance.

I acknowledge the large community of Police Officers, Community Service Officers, Department of Correction Officers, Public Safety Officers and Public Servants. Your exemplary dedication and service in your career and the commitment you make to public service does not go unnoticed. If you can save one life, you have done your job. Thank you for saving mine.

LAURA MITCHELL

CONTENTS

Acknowledgments viii

1 The Shackles 3

2 False Expectations 26

3 Don't Judge Me 41

4 Driven To Succeed 51

5 Reinventing Yourself 61

6 Create Opportunity 70

7 Handle Your Business 78

8 Just Say No 87

9 Love Yourself 95

10 Respect 104

11 Freedom 110

LAURA MITCHELL

CHAPTER 1

THE SHACKLES

I was twenty-three years old when I was sentenced to two years in the Colorado Women's Correctional Facility. I was the mother of two children under the age of three and had just found out I was pregnant with my fourth child.

I gave birth to my daughter on February 7, 1994 at St. Thomas Moore Hospital in Canon City, Colorado. I was shackled to a bed as I screamed.

The sun was shining through the glass of the cold van. I was being transferred from the prison to the local hospital. Inmates had to be brought through the back-door alley of the hospital. While in transition from the alley to the door, I was only allowed to stop during a contraction. I remember what a relief it was to breathe the fresh air and to have the cool breeze hit my face. The sun was a reminder that God was with me.

The nurse and doctor treated me as if I were invisible. They acted as if I were not in the room and in labor getting ready to give natural birth to a child. They never once looked me in the eye. The duo spoke only to the deputy who was assigned to me. Deputy Sarah Haynes. It was her job to get me to the hospital, hand the baby over to my parents, and get me back to my cell. I recall Deputy Haynes adjusting my shackles as they ripped into the side of my ankle with every contraction. The room was cold. I could smell bleach water and I watched a light bulb blinking in the ceiling fixture as I heard the deputy arguing with the doctor. She knew I was scared and in pain and she told him she was going to remove the shackle. He argued that it was out of protocol. As I heard the shackle hit the bedside, I felt the release of the metal latch and my foot fell free and I was able to give one good push to bring my baby into this world. It was a girl. I was relieved my daughter was healthy and I was filled with fear, not knowing when I would see her again.

The physical pain of natural childbirth was nothing compared to the pain I would feel when Deputy Haynes took my newborn baby into her arms and walked over to the bedside and let me get one last glimpse of my daughter's sweet face. I was in shock. I don't know if I held her; I only remember her big brown eyes. As the deputy walked through the door that led to freedom, where my parents were anxiously waiting, I screamed uncontrollably. I was at the lowest point in my life. Not once, but twice had I lost a child. In that moment of anger and disgust I made a decision. I would never allow myself to be in a helpless situation again. I made a decision to change.

When Deputy Haynes returned, I had already been restrained and returned to both shackles. She took me by the shoulders, looked me in the eyes, and said, "Hey, get it together! Everything is going to be okay. You are going to be okay. Your daughter is going to be okay." She repeated it over and over until I stopped screaming and crying. The doctor handed me a bag of menstrual pads and twenty minutes later I was back in a cell in the infirmary, childless, my womb was empty. I cried thinking to myself, this is not how it is supposed to be when you have child. I was placed in confinement for three days on suicide watch.

What they didn't know was that I did not want to die. I wanted to live. I finally wanted to live. I would never be shackled again.

Forgive Thyself

When I was released from the Women's Facility I returned to my parents' home. I was terrified of making a wrong decision. I would wake up in the middle of the night and pray to God to help me forget, and to help me focus on my dreams of becoming a better mother, daughter and sister. I would pray for God to give me the strength and the wisdom to face any obstacle that would come my way. All I could do was be accountable going forward.

I had become an embarrassment to myself and my family. I once overheard my brother say he didn't have a sister. I didn't blame him, he simply wanted to avoid answering questions about me, but his words hurt me badly.

I realized he had been under the spotlight and having to answer for my actions. My brother was right to deny me and avoid questions from friends and neighbors. My family had carried my burdens. I hurt so many people with my past choices. I lost their trust and all I could do was be accountable going forward.

I was released early from my sentence, three months after

my daughter was born. I was on a mission of mercy. I had endured more pain and suffering than some people endure in a lifetime. I was wiser and unstoppable. I was required to attend therapy and group counseling, and report once a week to my parole officer.

Enter Officer Maureen O' Connell. I liked to think of her as the female version of Samuel L. Jackson in Pulp Fiction. At our first meeting, she said to me, "I don't want to know what you did to get yourself in this mess. I want to know what you're going to do to move forward." Then she said the words I would live by for the next twenty-five years. "If you don't want to go back, don't look back!"

I never looked back. I figuratively swept this time in my life under the carpet until the writing of this book. Although after years of receiving and practicing counseling, I realize now this was not the best advice, but it was enough to keep me moving forward from my past.

My only mission was to get life my together. It was the only way I could restore my relationship with my family. The pain I caused people around me was deep. The pain I caused myself was deeper. I allowed the pain, guilt, and shame to become my drive. I realized that to move forward I had to forgive myself. Although it's been twenty-five years since the day I decided to get my life together, it was only this year that I wrote a forgiveness letter to myself because I was still struggling with my secrets. It turned into a love letter to me from me. I know it sounds ridiculous, but I added humor and only allowed positive statements. I took a good look at where I failed and what I could have done better. And because I was brave enough to evaluate my mistakes, I was able to find healing and forgive myself not just once, but throughout my life.

Matthew 18:21–22 (ESV) 21 Then Peter came up and said to him, "Lord, how often will my brother sin against me, and I forgive him? As many as seven times?" 22 Jesus said to him, "I do not say to you seven times, but seventy-seven times.

Clean Out Your Closet

A very dear friend once told me I needed to clean out my closet. If you know anything about me, you should know about the abundance of clothing in my closet. I'm going to be real right now and call it what it is: hope. I hope one day I will wear that size-four dress again.

Trust me, cleaning out your closet is not easy, but it is

necessary. There are things in there that you once loved and felt comfortable in. That old pullover was your best friend when you were feeling down. Your once favorite jeans hold the secrets to many places you should have never visited. Many of the items still fit, but they no longer represent who I am today. I definitely got rid of the clothing that was less forgiving to my hips, just like I got rid of the people that were less forgiving of my past. That sexy black dress? Leave it there, but please hold on to the Bon Jovi, Prince, and Lucky Charm T-shirts. I didn't say bury yourself. I said forgive yourself.

What you must know by now is that people can be cruel and hold grudges, and not everyone will forgive you. These are the people you need to remove from your life.

□

Thank You Very Much

I wasn't always a bad girl. I was raised by two hard working and loving parents. My mom worked at a local hobby store and my dad was a mailman. On Sundays we went to church, and afterward my dad worked on his truck in the garage, while my brothers and I played outside until sunset. We were what you would call back then a traditional family. In fact, I was never a "bad girl." I just made bad choices.

You may be recovering from a bad choice you made, or you may have done something that was out of your character and are looking for a way to move forward from a conviction. Conviction by the court, conviction of the heart, or conviction for the unforgiveness you may be holding on to. Perhaps you fell victim to drugs, alcohol, pornography, depression, or gambling, and have overcome those addictions. Maybe you let your emotions get the best of you in public or in private with someone you love, and you regret every word. That behavior is in the past, but while you were actively engaging in those things of the past, you were dragging people behind you, tormenting them with your actions. The people you hurt, the people you lied to, the people who were on your side—even if they didn't love you unconditionally - thank them.

This chapter is solely to acknowledge the people who loved and supported me. This chapter is to thank my brother for hurting me so deeply with his words, which made me bleed and seek wisdom to heal myself from my conviction.

This chapter is to thank my parents. My dad who defended me, never gave up hope, never left my side. He knew there was something greater in me. Thanks, Dad, for loving and reminding me that I was beautiful even when I was at my worst. My mom sacrificed her life's dreams and goals to take care of my children. She sacrificed her plans for me. There is no love greater than the love of a mother. Thank you, Momma.

This year after speaking at a conference, a woman who was sitting in the audience shared with me that she had been raising her granddaughter for four years because her son was incarcerated. She was so very angry at him and all she wanted him to do was acknowledge that her life was altered because of his decisions. I shared my story with her. I hugged her tightly and said, "Thank you." This woman walked away with great peace after telling me how she was ready to love him and support him.

Look in the Mirror

It took a long time for me to be able to stand in front of the mirror. It was a year after I was released from prison before I had a good stare-down with myself. Although I looked the same, I was not the same. I had just been through the wringer with reintegrating into society, parenting, and proving myself to everyone. I would look in the mirror and imagine I received a scholarship to the business school I would drive by each day. I imagined I was getting that promotion to a big office. I imagined I was already approved for a loan and moving into a 4,000-square-foot house. I imagined I was the CEO of a company. Any company. I was young, beautiful, and successful. I looked in the mirror and imagined myself getting into a convertible, any convertible, and driving off into the sunset.

At that time, I didn't know what CEO meant. Today, I am the Chief Executive Officer of two successful businesses. I found out that "CEO" means I get paid the most. Every day since then I look in the mirror, I strike my Wonder Woman pose, I tell myself I am blessed and highly favored and I encourage myself. I must admit, some days are better than others, but I still imagine myself living my dream. This morning, I imagined myself at my book signing.

At the time of this writing, the business is eighteen years young and I have three intelligent, savvy, talented partners—my children. You may be wondering; did she get the convertible? No, my life has changed dramatically since the fantasy about the convertible car. I've opted for more room to transport my groceries and decided keeping my hair intact is more important to me nowadays. Instead, I chose the AMG Crossover Sports Package.

The process of healing from your past doesn't happen overnight. I have been looking in that mirror for 25 years. It's okay to feel challenged, but do not feel sorry for yourself. Look in that mirror. Look at who you will become, not who you were. Here is some advice: no matter what you've done or where you are at this moment, get your butt up and keep moving toward your goal every single day. When you lay your head down at night, reflect only on the goodness of the day. Find something good. Thank God for where you are going.

Create an Affirmation for Yourself

No matter where you are in your healing process, if you really want to change your life and be successful you need to create an affirmation for yourself. Create something you can say to yourself when you are stressed or struggling, or simply say to yourself each day to remind yourself what you've been through and what you believe in. An affirmation allows you to reprogram your thinking. It can be a few words or an entire paragraph. You need to memorize your affirmation. Say it each day, when you wake up, at breakfast, lunch and dinner. When you are strong, and when you need strength.

I struggled with writing on this topic because I really don't have a grandiose affirmation or method on how to get one. At the time I wrote my first affirmation, I was just getting my life together, so I chose to focus on what I wanted to stay away from rather than where I was going. I simply condemned them from my life. I wanted it to sound so much more motivating and I wanted to sound so much smarter. I laugh out loud at myself now because all I could come up with was, "No man, no drink, no drug will keep me from the dream Jesus has in store for me."

It worked. There has not been a human in this world that I have let hold me back. There has not been a drink so tempting for me to thirst for while I was cleaning up, and there is not a drug in this world that can get me as high as my Jesus. These words got me through twenty-five years of sobriety and led me to a very successful life.

I have become a little wiser with maturity. I was able to organize my thoughts and upgrade my affirmation to the following: "Life has no limits, and anything is possible. I am good, I am kind, I am a giver. I will trust in the Lord. This is how I claim wealth and success."

To Dig Deeper, Answer The Following Question(s)

Have you truly forgiven yourself? If the answer is yes, simply write, I LOVE YOU. If the answer is no. It's time to forgive yourself so you can move forward. It's time to forgive anyone who has hurt you, so you can move forward, whether they forgive you or not. Forgiveness is for you.

Make a list here or in your thoughts about what you want to say to yourself. Be kind.

Dear _____,

Who do you need to thank for supporting you?

Who do you need to thank for loving you unconditionally?

Who do you need to thank that loved you with conditions?

Example: I love you, BUT you need to prove it to me by being to work 10 minutes early.

Let's clean out your closet. Do you have any old habits you need to clean out of your closet? Do you have friends that you need to say goodbye too?

Do you have a grudge you're holding on to?

Let's look in the mirror. You are absolutely amazing! Look at how far you have come! Pat yourself on the back. Is there somewhere you have always dreamt of visiting? Visualize yourself on that beach.

Is there something you really want at Target or Ikea? Visualize yourself putting that item in your cart and getting to the cash register only to find out it's half price.

Is it a relationship you're looking for? Visualize what you're going to wear on your date. Speak words of encouragement and success into the ears of that person in the mirror.

What is your affirmation? Let's get started!

SUCCESS UNSHACKLED

CHAPTER 2

FALSE EXPECTATIONS

When I was seventeen years old, I competed in the Miss Teen Colorado pageant. I performed a small skit from a dramatic play and was recognized by a local theater agent who offered me a full scholarship to the Boulder Theater Company. He said I captivated the audience and told me I was special. Later that year, I auditioned and was cast in a very popular soap opera. I graduated high school mid-year and moved to California to pursue an acting career. I didn't think twice when I took the role of the "maid's illegitimate daughter." I would be one of the first Latina/Hispanic actresses in Hollywood.

My parents were so proud of me. I had far exceeded my family's expectations for me to be the first one in our family to graduate from college. I was going to be a famous movie star in Hollywood. My family, teachers, neighbors, and coworkers were so excited for me and had a huge going-away party for me. Friends were asking for my autograph. I was expecting to finally get out of the west side of Denver, Colorado. It was no shocker that I was about to embark on a wild adventure. I was always the popular girl who had everything going for her. My world was about to change. When I arrived in Los Angeles it was a very exciting and unforgettable experience. It was a whole new world from how I was raised. I was the youngest person on the set and everyone loved me. I loved me, until I found out three months later I was pregnant by my high school sweetheart.

My family had no idea I was pregnant. I didn't have the heart to tell them I failed them, so I didn't. This was long before cell phones or social media. We still had to pay for long-distance calls on a landline. I could never find the words. I never really had a plan. I was just going to have my baby, and either they would accept me, or they wouldn't.

I figured everything would work itself out. I gave birth to a six-pound baby boy who I named Baby J. When he smiled, his little mouth was crooked, and his smile looked like a J. He was born with a critical congenital heart disease. He lived for twelve minutes. He died the day he was born in July 1987. It was the happiest and the saddest day of my life.

Fortunately, research and study of infants born with critical CHD began in the early nineties, and in 2004 screening tests for such diseases on unborn infants at 20 weeks was introduced. For more information on infant congenital heart disease screening, please talk to your physician or pediatrician.

I've never talked about the pregnancy, birth, or death until the writing of this book. I've never mentioned his name. I was numb inside. I was overwhelmed with shame, guilt, and anger. I was in shock. I had carried a child. He was alive and now he was gone.

We can go through life beating ourselves up over the false expectations that life delivers. I can tell myself, "I was supposed to be a famous movie star," or, "If only my son would have lived, I would have never made bad choices," or I can accept the fact that God had another plan for my life. The only expectations of my life are those I put on myself, to keep putting one foot in front of the other each and every day.

Things Are Not the Same

It was the fall of 1987, one month after I gave birth, I was eighteen years old when I resurfaced in the west side of Colorado. The studio released me. I was not famous, I had no explanation for my quick return from stardom. I had no explanation for my empty womb. I was lost. Nothing in my life would ever be the same, not now or ever. As time went by, I started smoking marijuana, using drugs, and drinking. It kept me numb from any thoughts I had about forfeiting my opportunities or losing my child. I was diligently working for prominent businesses. I was a smart girl but had no real focus for my life. I had just been offered an opportunity to go to Australia with the company I was working for when I found out I was pregnant with my second child. I was pregnant again at the door of opportunity. I turned down the invitation to Australia and I sobered up during my pregnancy. I tried hard to be excited and my family was supportive. My parents thought a baby would help me get my feet on the ground and turn things around. It would be a good second chance. When my son Jon was born, it was the second happiest day of my life. Jon was born at eight pounds and eight ounces. He was healthy. He would live.

I found yet another prominent organization to hire me,

each job better than the last. The opportunities were available by the handful. People seek opportunities like these their entire lives. Sadly, I still had no goals, focus, or vision. I was living WIC check to paycheck. Seventeen months later, I had my beautiful son Jeremy. He resembled Baby J. He was healthy. He would live. I wanted to die.

Clyde and I had known each other since the seventh grade. We became inseparable; he was my best friend. We laughed, we loved, and we had become one. We would separate but somehow, we always found our way back to each other. He was the father of my children. Clyde had my back and I had his. His name was fitting because we were like Bonnie and Clyde. For the younger generation, I was his Cookie and he was my Lucious. Not only were we in and out of love, we found ourselves in and out of trouble with the law. We were both drinking and drugging our way through the days. I made every attempt to stay numb.

One-night Clyde broke into an auto supply warehouse and abandoned our car with only two sets of fingerprints on the wheel, his and mine. Clyde was already on probation and would most likely serve prison time if he was caught. I feared my children growing up without a father, so I said it was me. I took the fall.

One morning I was on my way to check in to my monthly probation appointment with Officer Terry. She liked me and would go easy on me when I was a no-show or when I was late. She watched me struggle with my boys on and off the bus. I had missed two monthly appointments when I showed up at her doorstep that morning and she informed me I would not be leaving her office. She said there was nothing more she could do for me, I had violated my agreement with the State of Colorado, and my probation was revoked.

I was formally charged with Theft and sentenced to two years in the Colorado Women's Correctional Facility. As I lay in the bottom bunk of the cell in the infirmary, it was confirmed that I was pregnant. I would have my child inside the walls of The Colorado Department of Corrections. Yes, there was birth control in those days, but I didn't follow through with anything. I just didn't care.

Friends in Low Places

Do you ever notice that when you're feeling down and out, there's always someone there to celebrate your sorrows? These friends are usually the negative naysayers. You can talk to this friend but expect a negative answer. You can tell him or her that you won the lottery and they would say, "Man, now you have to pay taxes on it." I always find the one who says, "So what if it doesn't work out?"

These friends are in low places for a reason. They are most likely sulking around the shadows of who and what they could have been. When they go to sleep, they dream of yesterday or of nothing at all. They are going nowhere fast. You need to get away from them. Run. Run as fast as you can.

Friends in High Places

These are the people who you admire and trust. How much higher of a position can someone be in, other than being someone you trust? These friends will "Tony Robbins" your ass! They will hold you accountable with or without making you feel like a complete idiot. They will be on honest, listen to you, laugh with you, and cry with you.

Clyde and I eventually found our way back to each other, six months after my release from prison, but this time we were sober. We got married because we thought it was the right thing to do after what we had been through and because our children deserved to have a good life. We set out on a journey and were determined to provide our children with the best life possible. We set goals and when other people went to sleep to dream of a good life, Clyde and I stayed awake and created a life that people dream of. We had multiple businesses, expensive cars and large house on the top of the hill. Our children attended the best schools, had the latest shoes and gadgets that money could buy. We became very successful. Our marriage become superficial and materialistic. We were busy with our children and our careers didn't leave time for date night, so we showed love by presenting gifts to each other. We eventually lost each other somewhere in a purchase.

When I heard the rumor that Clyde was having an affair, I did what any woman does. I called my bestie Raney*. She answered the phone on the first ring and the moment I heard her voice I knew. I knew it was her. Raney was the one having an affair with my Clyde. She started to say I'm sorry and I became angry and screamed into the phone, "How could you do this to me?" She replied, "You should be happy it was me and not some stranger!" Those words made me feel as if the floor was falling from beneath me. I screamed at her and told her I was not going to let her get away with this! I was enraged with anger—not at him, but at her. Raney was someone I trusted with my children, my hopes, my dreams, and apparently, my husband. We spent birthdays and holidays together. Our kids were in Little League together. My heart pounded to the pace of my tears falling and I threw the phone across the room.

The next thing I remember I was sitting in my car in the parking lot of Raney's apartment complex. I was devastated just thinking about how she had deceived me. I thought about conversations we had, how she would ask if my husband was home or ask about our weekend plans. I felt so angry. I wanted to hurt her.

I had already made up my mind to run her over with my car when she came out of her apartment. There was no conviction, no thought of what would happen to my kids, nothing but laser-focus on my goal. This was it. As I sat outside the apartment complex, humped over my steering wheel, my phone rang. I thought maybe it was Raney and I would lure her outside. Instead it was another friend, Sally*. Sally had already heard the news and asked me what I was doing, so I told her. Sally lived two blocks away from Raney and she said, "Girl, you stay right there and don't make a move."

Sally was panting as she kept talking to me, and before I

knew it, Sally threw herself on the front of my car. At first, I thought I had stepped on the gas and I had really hit Raney with my car, but then I noticed the person on the hood was Sally. When I got out of the car, I watched Sally slide off the hood of my car and I noticed that she was only wearing her socks. I said "Sally, did you just run two blocks in socks?" She came over to my car door and we laughed hysterically. Then I cried in her arms. It was the love of a true friend that saved me from myself. Sally saved me from becoming a savage.

Sally has always found the best in people. She is a very fun, loving, and humble woman who has devoted her life to caring for children, her family, and friends.

She is my hero. I recognize her as one of my most valuable friends in the highest arenas of my life. She is one friend I can call any time, day or night. No matter how much time has passed between us, she'll always tell me the truth. If she can't help me, she knows someone who will. She is an encourager and has always found the best in people.

This experience helped me recognize that I needed to set a higher standard for myself and for the people I allow into my life. I needed to respect myself and those I have relationships with. Things happen in relationships; disagreements, lack of communication, and so on, but when you respect each other it's that much easier to overcome any misunderstanding. I just don't have one best friend. I have a circle of loving, trusting, and faithful relationships. We evaluate our friendship by asking one another, "Would I run two blocks in my socks for you?"

To Dig Deeper, Answer The Following Question(s)

Write down a time when an outcome was different from your expectation? What did you learn from that?

Make a list of some changes that you would like to make in your life. Put a timeline to the items on your list. Be accountable to yourself.

Do you have a Sally in your life? There is no time to get the keys, no time to get shoes. Do you have anyone that would run two blocks in their socks for you?

Do you have anyone that you would run two blocks in your socks for?

LAURA MITCHELL

CHAPTER 3

DON'T JUDGE ME

This is my hang-up. It wasn't until recently that I realized that the fear of being judged was the sole reason that kept me from conquering the universe and obtaining absolutely everything I could possibly dream of. It makes me angry to think that I could have been further along in my life if I didn't have that inner voice telling me I wasn't good enough or that I would be judged.

It took some good soul-searching along with a few sessions of therapy to find out when and where those lying voices came from. When I was about seven years old, I helped my aunt put away the groceries. She didn't like the way I handled the bread, so she grabbed it from my hands and said something about me in Spanish. It was a word I didn't recognize but from the tone, her actions, and, simply, the way it made me feel, it embedded the feeling of unworthiness and fear of being judged. I let that silly moment in time define me. The fact that I didn't even know what the word meant made it worse. I grew up thinking I wasn't good enough. I later learned that the word meant "stupid."

I was constantly afraid of being judged. That same fear arose again when I came home from Hollywood—not a star, but a complete failure. I let people believe I wasn't good enough. I let them judge me because it was easier than telling everyone my business, and I eventually believed it. It kept me from getting my life together. I had great jobs, but I didn't believe I was good enough to succeed any higher. I settled for mediocre because I was safe there. No one judges mediocre.

Expect It

I had already known how to live with the feeling of being judged, but now it was different. I had just been released from prison and I really was being judged for my choices, my character, and my conviction. I expected to be turned down for a job because of my conviction. Now, I really wasn't good enough.

I didn't realize I was in a cycle of allowing my past and inner thoughts to control me. I was secretly and deathly afraid of being judged. I hid from myself for over twenty years and I became very good at it.

When I was finally able to face my fear and I no longer expected judgement but accepted it, I began to release those shackles of unworthiness that I had carried around for far too long. I began to say, "I'm sorry," "thank you," and "I love you" to myself.

Perception

I believe that I am a very beautiful woman. For most of my life, I have taken good care of myself. I exercise, I make a great effort to get up every morning, put on my makeup, get dressed, and be ready for the day. I don't leave the house without looking in the mirror and affirming myself. People often comment on how they rarely see me not dressed for any occasion. I take pride in myself and represent myself as the daughter of a King. I'm often perceived as having at it all together.

Did you hear me? I said, "I make a great effort" and am "often perceived of having it all together," but it doesn't happen every day. I hate to get up in the morning. I cannot move forward with my day without coffee. I hate to floss, and I dread the hour it takes to put makeup on. My closet constantly looks like the entire cast of Hamlet changed in there. I love to sleep on my face and my side and wear a grubby T-shirt and sweats and eat peanut butter out of the jar while I watch the Today Show. I don't usually make any guest appearances on those days.

This is who I am in the privacy of my own home. I'm human. When I get onstage and I tell my story, I want to deliver a real and truthful message of how I have overcome, that no matter how I am perceived by others, it doesn't matter to me. I know who I am and what I am capable of. I love me.

If you have ever heard the words, "you aren't good enough", "you aren't capable", or "you are stupid." I need you to dig down deep, pull that moment in time from your soul, and release that shackle of lies into the universe and the heavens above.

Answer Their Questions

Be prepared to answer any question you may encounter regarding your past. I have found that unless you are speaking to a true friend or someone in recovery, it is best to keep your answer simple. Save your life story for someone who will recognize you for who you are today.

My favorite question is, "Is it true your husband cheated on you with your best friend?" I want to scream out loud, "I was in prison, people, and this is what you want to know?" So, I take a deep breath and answer the question with a calm and collective spirit. People can be so cruel. They can be nosy and downright rude. They are usually the "perfect ones." Insert "laugh out loud" here. Nevertheless, answer the question, be accountable for your past actions, allow them to see God in you, allow them to see your pain and your victory.

"You Look Familiar"

One of my clients going through addiction counseling would tell a story about how he felt when someone said to him, "You look familiar." He said he would literally go into panic mode. Did he pick a fight with them? Did he sleep with them? Did he owe them money? Did he know them from jail? This resonates with me because I do the same. I've been through hell and I'm on my way to heaven. I have been places that I am ashamed of, and I have been places that I never dreamed of. Yes, I may look familiar. Roll with it. If they remember you from a good time, claim it, smile, laugh out loud because they remembered you. If it's from a less noble time, claim it, apologize, smile, thank God that He brought you through it. If it's not you and it's truly is a case of mistaken identity, claim it, introduce yourself, embrace crossing the path of someone new.

Humility

When I was 30 years old and somewhere between the college classes, running the business and raising the kids, I began to feel overwhelmed. I had become so busy and focused on succeeding in every aspect of my life that I was no longer concerned with making a difference; I was about getting the job done. I noticed myself becoming very demanding and controlling. I wanted things done quick, fast and right now, if it someone couldn't provide the results, I wanted I would get them myself. In conversation, I became quick to answer and slow to listen. I was exhausted.

There was a still small voice nudging at me daily, telling me to slow down and take a good look at my life. I was becoming arrogant. I slowed down long enough to see that my insecurities had surfaced. I could not find any balance and didn't have time to be humble.

I was working so hard to prove myself to everyone. I was anxious because I had stopped attending therapy. I was empty because I hadn't volunteered in months. I decided I didn't want to be this person anymore. How could I possibly change now?

I decided I would take on one simple task: I would keep my mouth shut.

I would not voice my demands, I would not give my opinions. I would see what others were capable of without my guidance. Just this one task humbled me like no other. When I shut up, I was able to see the smart, talented, and amazing people God put into my life. I was able to hear new ideas and solutions, and the best thing of all was that I renewed my outlook on life.

I was absolutely humbled by just listening to my surroundings and being in the moment. I began to want to serve, to cherish moments, and to make an honest difference. I was still highly assertive, but I was also equally intuitive. People can change.

☐

To Dig Deeper, Answer The Following Question(s)

Have you ever been judged based on your race, religion or simply your looks?

Have you ever been judged based on your past?

What did you do about it?

What would you have done differently about it?

How do you think you are perceived by people?

Is this the image you want your children and grandchildren to remember you?

What can you do to work on your image?

LAURA MITCHELL

CHAPTER 4

DRIVEN TO SUCCEED

The day I watched the security guard carry my baby girl out of the birthing room door in the hospital, something deep inside me shifted. That was the moment I made a decision. One single decision. I was determined to never find myself in that situation again. I would never again be shackled.

I was driven to succeed at everything I could get my hands on. I was driven to become a great mother, a contributing member of society, a friend, a counselor, and a witness to what the Glory of God looks like. That feeling of loss, disgust, disbelief, anger, and shame is what changed me that day. One single decision was my tool.

There have been hundreds of people I have crossed paths

51

with that I have been able to help ease the pain of an addiction, fear, or loss. I have provided hope or healing because of the power of my testimony. This is what drives me to get out of bed every single morning.

When I place my feet on solid ground each day, the devil knows I am awake and alive, and I make sure that he hears me give thanks and all the glory to God with each stretch into the new day. All I have to do is put one foot in front of the other, for God has already ordered my steps.

☐

Don't Look Back

Over the years, I created my own rules. I avoided any kind of judgment from anyone. I let my dominant personality trump any thought of not being good enough, and I was out to prove the world wrong. I was good enough, but I would back down from any situation where someone made me prove my worth. As powerful as I had become in my community and as a successful entrepreneur, I still feared being judged on any level. Was I handling the bread carefully enough? Was I doing everything with care? Although, my children were college educated and exceptional human beings and I was a counselor at church. I had been married to my first husband for almost twenty years and had an amicable divorce. I was educated, held several key executive positions in my professional career, and I remarried an amazing, honorable man. God had kept His word and given me a second chance.

The words "if you don't want to come back, then don't look back" were embedded in my mind, and it's true. I certainly didn't want to suffer so for many years. I didn't look back and eventually I began to forget where I came from. Besides, why would any successful person ever want to look back? My life had become predictable, comfortable, and safe.

I began to feel like I was not doing enough. I had a void. Something deep inside me said I had more to give. That still-small voice inside me said I had to look back.

☐

What Others Don't Know

As a therapist, I have counseled individuals and couples for several years. I have presented at small group seminars, I teach on occasion at the local community college, and I conduct behavioral health evaluations for one of the largest airlines in the world. I convinced myself that if I was the judge or authority in charge, this would not give anyone an opportunity to form an opinion about me or to judge me. I was smart, worthy, and capable. I am excellent at one-on-one therapy, but I doubted myself when it came to speak on stage. I wanted to reach more people at once. I wanted to teach people about healthy relationships, and I wanted to become a better speaker.

I signed up for a seminar in Fort Lauderdale, Florida. It was titled "Master the Mic." Fair enough. It was exactly what I wanted, and I had never been to Florida. The seminar was hosted by one of the world's best motivational speakers, Les Brown, and his family. I loved Les Brown and figured I could use a little motivation in my life.

Little did I know that weekend would change my life. From the moment I entered that room I knew I would never be the same. It was a safe environment. Love, joy, and excitement filled the air. As we all introduced ourselves, I realized the room was filled with people who all had a story. I felt out of place. I was just there to become a better speaker to promote my profession. I wasn't there to put all my business on the table. I was vulnerable.

We were given a class assignment. Attendees were asked to line up to get on the stage. The person in front of them was asked to give the person behind them a word or topic on which to give a two-minute speech. My word was "freedom."

I didn't have much time to contemplate what I was going to say about this single word that defined my life. My palms were sweating, and my knees were shaking as I began to hear stories of recovery and redemption. Before I knew it, there I was standing on that stage, vulnerable and ready to break free from my past. I told my story about how I gave birth to my daughter twenty-five years ago while I was shackled to a bed in prison. I shared stories of my success and how I moved forward one step at a time. It was there in that conference room that I looked back and was set free from the shackles that kept me from moving forward. God wasn't done with me yet. He was just getting started.

Lost Talents

I grew up thinking I wasn't capable of handling a loaf of bread. Then other events in my life added to that negative thinking, and I let the fear of judgment allow me to forget my worth.

When I was seventeen years old, I was great on that pageant stage where I revealed my acting talent. I captivated audiences. Today, I am not acting, this is me. I am great, I am powerful, I am worthy, I am wise, and I am a force to be reckoned with.

My testimony of courage, love, and forgiveness captivates hearts and heals souls.

God is not finished with you yet!

To Dig Deeper, Answer The Following Question(s)

What drives you to get up in the morning?

What is that still small voice saying to you?

How will you answer it?

What moment in your life defines who you are today?

Are you on your path of purpose?

What are your lost talents?

Do you have something inside you that you can share?

Do you have a story to tell that only you can tell?

CHAPTER 5

REINVENTING YOURSELF

When I started this chapter all I could do was think of Les Brown when he talked about how much he loves sweet potato pie and peanut butter M&Ms, and how he has lost twenty pounds several times.

I have loved deeply and have reinvented myself. Several times. When I got out of prison. When I divorced my husband. When I became a single parent. When I was able to become a friend again. When I started a new career. When I married again. And when I became a motivational speaker and author.

I'm not going to give you a bunch of bull about how easy it was. It wasn't. It stinks.

There are no directions and there is no empathy involved. Reinventing yourself takes time and courage.

When I was in my twenties and getting my life back together after incarceration, it was much easier to start over. Youth was on my side and I had much more energy. I leaned heavily on surrounding myself with good, positive people who had goals. I had several mentors in whom I could confide and ask for advice.

After my divorce, I had to focus first on my finances and make sure I could sustain a lifestyle I was comfortable with. I cut back, cut up my credit cards and sold off the material things I could live without. I soon realized I had to take care of myself for myself. I looked at my health plan and started taking care of my body. I began exercising right there in the front of the iPad until I got up the courage to go back into the world and join a gym. I started eating better. I cut and colored my hair. I'm not saying you should do this but let me tell you it felt good to make the physical changes. I started volunteering and began to rebuild my spirit by engaging in serving others. Some days were better than others. It was all very hard and lonely. I kept going, I kept praying, I kept thinking about praying, and eventually I started to see progress in my life. At the end of the day it was just me, myself, and I.

Slowly, life started to happen around me. I started dating while still working through the semantics of being a single mom. The kids and I had to discover a new normal in the household, but I was so guilty about the divorce that I stopped disciplining and tried to become a friend to my teenage kids. This was a huge mistake. They needed a parent more than ever. We learned to be honest with each other about our feelings and communicate our expectations and set new boundaries for our new life.

After being deceived by my closest friend, I began to let a few trusted people back into my life. With each experience and reinvention, I began to raise my standards. I ventured out into a new profession and again, I had to continue to establish good habits for myself, like going back to school, working out regularly, and simple things like going to bed at a decent hour.

My biggest reinvention was when I got married again. To reinvent myself as a wife, I had to take a good, honest look at my first marriage and ask myself what I could have done differently. Where did I fall short of meeting his needs? I asked these questions of the past relationship to help me develop new questions for my future. How will I be his helpmate and his companion? How does he hear love? I had to be willing to let go of my selfish needs and become selfless.

I will forever be reinventing myself as a speaker and author. It's a surreal and humbling experience to share your life story with a stranger and have them relate in some way to your pain and victory.

Help Me

During the reinvention process I realized how much I didn't know about life. Who knew the car battery is now in the trunk of some cars instead of under the hood? I certainly did not. I had to humble myself to myself when it came to be asking for help. At all the stages of reinventing myself I did this. It really is true that it's not what you know, but who you know. Each time I opened myself up to asking for help I met the most amazing people. I am thankful, and I cherish my experiences with people.

My life, knowledge, and career opportunities typically left me feeling pretty savvy about life until I met an exceptional category of people: military spouses. If you ever need to know how, what, where, why, statistics, and facts about any subject in the world just ask a military spouse. They are the strongest, smartest, most amazing people you will ever meet. Their experience supporting their spouse while deployed or through the chaos of moving their family around the world every two—four years is commendable. I am proud and honored to serve and stand by their side, as they have accepted and loved me unconditionally.

When asking for help, the best advice I have is to be kind to one another and to remember that you have great value and knowledge to share also.

Community

My separation and divorce were public because we were advisors, mentors, and had a significant presence in our community. It was difficult for me, my children, and my staff to have people come into our place of business and offer their thoughts of empathy for our family. No one died, but it sure felt like it. My children and I grieved as if there were a death. As humiliating as it felt for us at that time, I look back and I can still see the faces of the individuals from the community that meant well; people brought us food, coffee, and a few of my clients brought wine. Prayer warriors came to pray for and with us. My most dedicated clients and friends made financial donations to the organization until I could figure things out. Community comes together in times of need without judgment and with love and support.

Gain Some New Knowledge

I want to make something clear: reinventing yourself doesn't have to follow trauma or a life crisis. You can make a decision right now to add to your life, change your life, or gain new knowledge. There are too many resources out there to list that will allow you to learn and experience new adventures in your lifetime. You can literally type your thoughts into a search engine and new information is at your fingertips. When I decided to write this book and share my hardships and triumphs with the world, I learned that every person I talk to either knows someone or has a family member who has had some sort of victory over their battles with addiction, cancer, depression, gambling, anxiety, suicide, or fear, and they, too, have a story. I learned how much work, effort, and commitment it takes to write a book, but the best thing of all is that I finally learned how to navigate through documents, share files, and where the downloaded document really goes.

☐

To Dig Deeper, Answer The Following Question(s)

What decision can you make TODAY to put yourself on the path you want to be on?

How often do you volunteer? Write it down. Be accountable to yourself.

What is one thing you are interested in learning about?
How can you go about educating yourself?

CHAPTER 6

CREATE OPPORTUNITY

In this chapter I want to talk about creating opportunity by facing your fears. The fear of judgment was so powerful in my life that instead of simply facing my fears and letting go of what people would think or say about me, I held on to the lie that I wasn't good enough and as a result I worked so much harder than I had to. I put myself through the wringer trying to avoid any embarrassment to myself or my family after having been incarcerated. I created my own opportunity but at the cost of my health, my first marriage, and my spirit. Don't let your fears steal your time from you. Don't let your fears keep you from your dream.

Each time I speak about my experiences or I get up on a stage to share my victory, I think about how much time I wasted giving into my fear of being judged. I think about how many people I could have encouraged sooner. I think about how many young girls are lost with no hope, having babies in prison and just needing to hear that everything will be okay. I think about how I could have been providing therapy to a mother grieving her child. Fear had my opportunity shackled in its possession for over twenty years. I have taken it back and I have created my own opportunity today. Judge away.

Do Your Research

Facing your fear is the first step in creating your opportunity. No matter what you are afraid of, don't let it hold you back from moving forward.

One of the very first times I shared my story, a young lady came up to me in tears and told me that my message spoke directly to her. She had just finished school and wanted to apply for a better job but was embarrassed because she had a conviction. She was told by her school employment counselor that she wasted her time taking classes and she didn't have a chance. I advised her to visit the company website or to call and ask about the qualifications for the job. I encouraged her to apply, be confident, be prepared to answer any questions, and be honest in her interview.

She emailed me a week later to tell me she received an offer for employment.

Trust Your Instincts

From my experience, I believe you should you never doubt your instincts. Call it your gut, call it the Holy Spirit Itself, but never doubt your instincts. Don't rest or debate on this feeling. If it feels right, go for it! If it feels wrong, run as fast as you can, as far as you can.

Now, I am not talking about going about the day just doing whatever you feel like. Please use discernment and your common sense. There were several times in my life I wish I would have obeyed my intuition instead of taking a loss or wasting precious time. Who knows where God would have taken me?

☐

If It Sounds Too Good to Be True...

Because we as human beings have been taken advantage of or don't find ourselves worthy, we find ourselves working for less money or paying higher interest on loans because of credit problems. We tell ourselves "It's okay, it was a good deal," or "I didn't have a choice because of my divorce," and so on. If it sounds too good to be true it probably is. This is when you need to realize your worth. Your new reinvented worth. Learn to not be in a hurry when faced with a decision or offer of any kind. Weigh your options, ask questions, ask for references. If you are trying to increase your credit score by utilizing a higher interest credit card or loan offer, then yes, some programs are put in to place to assist in re-establishing credit, but have a plan to pay that high-interest card off as soon as possible. If you are not savvy about finances, ask questions, ask for references to direct you. If you finally land that dream opportunity but it's only available during the hours that you normally attend your child's recital or practice, ask yourself if it's as good as it sounds? You cannot get those precious moments back.

Whenever I am drawn into something that I think will be as good as it sounds, I remind myself, "You don't live like that anymore." My worth has tripled over the last five years, having this attitude.

Ask God to give you the wisdom to make a good choice that will benefit your future.

Career Options

Most people have an idea or dream of what they wanted to be when they grew up. I wanted to work everywhere and do everything. My dad always told me I could do anything I wanted to. So I did.

I have had several opportunities in my life and with each one I thought, this is it, this is my spot in the world. But no matter where or which job I landed, it was never enough for me. I never felt accomplished. It was because God was preparing me to share my story with the world, with homemakers, service clerks, with career professionals, with teachers, preachers, and presidents. He allowed me to relate to all walks of life, to be used only as a mirror and a messenger of hope. If I could overcome the pain of my past, so can you.

I have proudly worked as a sales clerk, a cook, a receptionist, an office manager, elementary teacher, child care administrator, minister, therapist, and a college teacher. I've worked in the movie industry, airline industry, at a newspaper, a magazine, and was a vice president in the corporate world. I am most recently a CEO, entrepreneur, speaker, and author. My success has finally been unshackled, and I have found my place. Whatever your career options are, strive to be fulfilled.

☐

To Dig Deeper, Answer The Following Question(s)

What is holding you back from doing what you were born to do?

What can you do to move past this? What have you already decided to do?

☐

CHAPTER 7

HANDLE YOUR BUSINESS

You are responsible for you. If you have children, they will grow up someday and they will be responsible for themselves. If you have a husband, he is not responsible for you. He is responsible for himself.

If you decide to move forward from a mistake or tragedy you long to overcome, then you must take full responsibility for your actions, your thoughts, your words, and your decisions. You must be able to handle your own business. You must speak up. You must stand up for yourself. You must challenge yourself, and you must trust yourself.

Honor Your Word

If you have been deceived, then you know what it feels

like to lose trust. The only thing that will make you feel better and begin to help you heal from deception or pain is forgiveness. If you choose to continue to seek recovery in that relationship, then you must forgive the person who lied or let you down. Set boundaries for yourself and let them know your expectations and that you need them to be accountable, so you do not get hurt again. You have already decided to forgive this person and move forward. Honor your word. Do not go back and seek revenge through anger, hatefulness, or verbal abuse. Honor your word and your decision to move forward, trusting and challenging yourself to forgive. When you honor your word, you build character. Character defines us.

If you have deceived someone, perhaps lied or committed an act outside of your character that you need to apologize for, you must first forgive yourself. Take full responsibility for your actions. Humble yourself. Remember you are the one who caused the pain, you are the one asking for a second chance. Expect consequences, be accountable. Do what you say you are going to do, be where you say you are going to be, and make every effort to be forgiven. Apologize and make amends. Honor your word.

Become a Timekeeper

This simple task helps us handle the business of life effectively. Time is so very valuable. I'm not referring to setting up a checklist with a time slot. I'm referring to how you are spending your time. Have you become so busy that you don't have time to stop and smell the roses?

It's your life. Will you take the time out of your week to spend nurturing a relationship? When was the last time you had lunch with your best friend? When was the last time you called someone you love and really listened? Put the phone down and have a conversation with a teenager, who may desperately need the social interaction. Be a timekeeper for the quality of your life.

Tell the Truth

There is nothing more powerful than looking someone in the eye when you have something to say and telling the truth. It wasn't until the writing of this book that I shared my story in its entirety with close friends and family. I never discussed the loss of my baby or having my daughter in prison. I didn't lie. I just didn't say anything. I figured if no one really knew my past, they couldn't judge me, and I would be good enough for whatever role I was in.

Many people debate about telling the truth. Personally, I feel like no matter what you have been through and no matter how hard it is, it's not rocket science: if someone can't accept you for who you are, then they shouldn't be in your life anyway. When you tell the truth, you are free. Free to tell the story of your life, free to display your weaknesses and strengths. Yes, the truth will set you free from the tangled web of lies you have weaved, but you must remember that it takes some time to unravel that mess. You will be vulnerable to getting your feelings hurt, losing a few friends, and maybe even nailed to the cross for judgment. It can be painful, but you are no longer the one causing the pain.

The topics discussed range from, it's ok to tell a white lie, and it's ok to lie if you save someone from getting hurt. You need to make a conscious decision about what will come out of your mouth and what you can live with.

Family and Friends

I stay consistent with my belief to love thy neighbor, and to be kind and compassionate with friends and family, but I stand firm on my belief that we can choose the people we let into our lives. You need to have standards for yourself and to be respected. Bishop T.D. Jakes says, "Do not pour yourself into people who do not pour into you."

I was having a conversation with my mother about social media and how amazing it is to stay in touch and up to date with cousins, friends, coworkers, and neighbors. We were able to reminisce about the good ole' days, laugh at my crazy cousin and his outrageous posts, share my daughter's wedding pictures, and send birthday wishes to our friends in Korea. We are thankful for the technology that has allowed us to appreciate family and true friends.

My mom said that every time she hits the "like" button it's like giving hug. In that moment with my mom, I hugged her. Cherish your time.

☐

To Dig Deeper, Answer The Following Question(s)

What can you do to make sure you are being responsible and accountable?

Are you following through with your commitments?

Do you honor your word? How?

Do you have a mobile or physical calendar that you look at every day?

Are you following through with your appointments and commitments?

Is there something you are holding on to confessing? It's time to come clean and be accountable. Sit silently and look at the lines on the paper and think about what you would say. Pray and ask God for wisdom.

Let's test your accountability: Make a to-do list here for the week with today's date. Write in your calendar 10 days from today's date "check my to do list in Success Unshackled" page no. _____. You'll let yourself know if you are accountable.

LAURA MITCHELL

CHAPTER 8

JUST SAY NO

From my professional and personal experience, individuals in recovery of any topic, deal with feelings of guilt and the need to prove ourselves credible. We don't want to say no, but very quickly, we find ourselves involved in other affairs before we come into our own healing. In my personal life, I found myself saying yes to everything. I had three children in three to six different activities a week, I was going to church, school, running a business and trying to keep my marriage together. I was becoming depressed because I had no time for myself. Unfortunately, the day I finally said no was a day when I was less gracious than I had ever been, I had a complete melt down right there at the counter in the grocery store when I realized I was wearing two different shoes. From that moment forward, I began to say no. I went through my calendar, highlighted my priorities and politely cancelled and declined any invitation or task outside of my priorities. I felt relief.

One of my dearest colleagues, Mrs. Barbra Russell, wrote a book titled Yes! I Said No! which is an entire book on saying no. I had to read it twice to absorb the value of the concept.

☐

Ask Not, Have Not

James 4:2 says, "Ye have not, because ye ask not."

The first time I heard the words, "Those who ask not have not" I was literally brought to my knees. It is your God-given right to ask. We are entitled because it is written in His word. Ask from a place of humility, ask kindly, ask humbly for what is already yours. God expects us to ask!

I recommend using discretion and discernment when talking to people you do not know, but don't be afraid to ask for something. When you are child and your parents tell you no, you keep asking and asking, and asking until eventually you get it or in some cases oftentimes, the answer is no and stays that way. This is ok too. You can have peace knowing you asked and learn to appreciate what you do have.

When you are an adult and already set in your ways, one of the hardest things we must do is ask.

I have received hotel upgrades, airline upgrades, complimentary tickets, front-row parking, complimentary oil changes, and refunds simply by asking. I have received favor on deadlines and better interest rates.

I never say I get something "for free." It's not a favor if it's expected to be returned. I say it's complimentary, because it is it compliments of my Lord and Savior who already paid in full. I don't get everything I ask for, but I am mindful about what I put out into the universe. If I don't receive the upgrade I ask for, I walk away with a heart of thanksgiving. I no longer fear rejection.

But God exceeded my expectations when I began to ask for the things in life that really matter. I was so very lonely and had been on dates with men with whom I was incompatible. I wanted someone to share my life with. I prayed for a man who was honorable. I prayed that he would send someone who was equally yoked to my maturity, level of education, and authority. Someone who had already acquired stability. I asked God to let him to have a sense of humor and, at the very least have his own parking space with his name on it. God says to pray specifically, right?

The day this man pulled up to his parking space in front of the building with his name on it, I'm pretty sure I shouted out loud, "Thank you, Jesus!" to the heavens above. This was my man. Forget about a parking space, this man had an entire building with his name on it. Exceeding, abundantly, and beyond measure does He give you what you ask for.

John 16:23 says, "And in that day ye shall ask me nothing. Verily, verily, I say unto you, Whatsoever ye shall ask the Father in my name, he will give it you."

Don't Settle

I get myself into trouble with this one. I have had to learn to pick and choose my battles when it comes to this one. Let's say I get the wrong coffee order and I have already left the building. I don't necessarily want this drink that I paid good money for, but I weigh out my options and my time, I decide, and I move forward. I don't consider this settling.

Now, my husband I are on two opposing teams when it comes to this. If he orders a well-done burger and it comes to the table medium, he would just eat it. It wasn't what he wanted, but he didn't want to put anyone out of their way to fix the problem, and he walks away unhappy and feeling like he settled. Now with me, on the other hand, they are going to have to make it right. I don't need an apology. I just want them to make it right. When I want something a certain way, I have learned to voice my expectations and be very specific in the service I want, especially if I pay for a service. Only when I know that I have no control over a situation can I be comfortable with the outcome and accept it without feeling like I settled. I don't want to be superior to anyone or anything, but life is too short to settle. I know my worth and I know that I am born for greatness. With this attitude I have had to learn to be patient and to handle any in discrepancies with kindness and order.

Worst-Case Scenario

The worst-case scenario is death. If you are not in a casket, then every second of every day you still have an opportunity. Trust yourself.

☐

To Dig Deeper, Answer The Following Question(s)

When was the last time you said yes? When was the last time you said no?

Do you have healthy boundaries between the yes and no commitments?

Are you making any settlements in your life? Why?

What can you do to not accept anything less than you deserve?

LAURA MITCHELL

CHAPTER 9

LOVE YOURSELF

In 2015 I was in the best shape of my life. I was at the top of the chain in the corporate world, I was traveling, and I had just met the love of my life. I finally felt like my life was coming along wonderfully. I had decided it was time to spend some time and money on myself. I visited a plastic surgeon to inquire about having a breast reduction. I had been unhappy with my body and I was self-conscious about the size of my breasts since I was a young girl. I was determined to finally be happy about the size of my breasts no matter the cost.

The surgeon took one look at me, told me how lucky I was, and refused to provide the service. But I was determined to get my way. I visited another surgeon who agreed to the surgery, but during the exam found a lump in my left breast and referred me to my primary care doctor. I had not had a routine checkup. After a mammogram and several tests including a biopsy, I was diagnosed with breast cancer. I was in shock hearing the words. I was scheduled for surgery the following day. As I listened to the doctor giving me facts and options for surgery, there was a chance for a full or partial loss of my left breast. I remember holding my hands across my chest and crying out loud, "Please God, I'm sorry, please don't take my girls!"

My daughter, who had been my sidekick her entire life, immediately became my kickstand. She delivered the good news to me that the doctors were able to remove the cancer and my breast would be missing tissue, but they would be fully intact. Following radiation, I recovered quickly. I am so thankful I was able to keep my girls. I am no longer embarrassed or unhappy about my body. I am blessed.

My message here is to love yourself just the way you are and to take care of yourself. Whether you are male or female, make it a point to have a routine visit with your physician. Early detection is a large factor in increasing the survival rate in patients diagnosed with breast cancer.

Establish a Support System

When something goes wrong, you typically call your mother or your best friend. Except in my case, I was blindsided when I found out my best friend was having an affair with my husband. My support system just collapsed. My mother was just as devastated as I was. Now she needed a support system, too.

So, I did what any normal human would do. I shut down and started feeling sorry for myself. Then the depression kicked in, along with the occasional visit from the suicide demons. I knew I had to do something, but I could no longer trust anyone. Everyone in my life had just deceived me. I had already overcome so many hardships in my life. I started thinking about my children. I had to be strong for them, and I made a promise to never leave them again. I had to get myself together. I hit my knees one night and asked God for strength, I made a decision to get some help. One decision. I reached out to a beloved friend and she rushed to my side, got me to a hospital, to a church, and into counseling. I was able to meet people who were on a path to recovery and healing. I developed a support system with skilled individuals who inspired me to raise my standards, individuals who valued me, respected me, and challenged me. That one decision to get help set me on my professional path to study psychology and become a counselor.

Find an Outlet

At one time I thought my children were my outlet and then I discovered they were the reason I needed an outlet. I began to walk around the local park, and then I began to run. It made me feel good. I started sleeping better and running helped me feel accomplished. I challenged myself to run a 5k race, then a half-marathon. I don't know what I was thinking with that one. By mile ten I started writing my will in my head. I thought that decision was for sure going to be the death of me. I lived and have a gorgeous medal to prove it. Running is still my outlet, on my time, at my pace. It gives me time to think, sometimes pray, but always makes me feel good about myself. Find something you enjoy. I have a friend who is the CEO of a sporting goods label, and his outlet is to crochet. He's not good enough to sell anything he makes, but he finds great peace in working that yarn.

Feed Yourself

This is important.

In addition to your outlet, find time to educate yourself. If you are reader, make a commitment to read something inspirational, positive, or motivating daily. No excuses. There are phone apps that will read to you. Remember the genius words of Dr. Seuss:

"The more that you read, the more things you will know. The more that you learn, the more places you'll go." — Dr. Seuss

I have experienced tremendous growth in my life since I began to venture out and attend seminars, workshops, and classes. If you feed yourself, believe in yourself, challenge yourself, and trust yourself, you will see anything is possible. For me, this book is proof of that. Someday, we can have dinner together when my first TED Talk is posted on social media.

☐

To Dig Deeper, Answer The Following Question(s)

Make a list of 5 things you can do to take care of yourself, outside of your normal routine. Make it good! This is to you, from you. Find a way to put this list into play. Make the time. You are worth it!

What is your outlet? Write it down and explain why this is your outlet? How does it make you feel?

What does your support system look like?

In the event of an emergency who will you call?

In the event that you have an extra concert ticket, who will you call?

☐

What are you investing your time in? What are you reading or listening to today? Can you legitimately write it down on this page?

What is in your playlist? What was the last thing you watched on social media? Did it fuel you in any way?

CHAPTER 10

RESPECT

Respect is deep admiration for someone because of their abilities, qualities or achievements. This is you! You have the ability to accept responsibility for yourself, your qualities are valued, and you far exceed the recognition you give yourself for what you have achieved thus far in life. Because of where I have been and the fact that I know I am a product of God's grace, I will never again allow anyone to treat me like I am invisible, insignificant or that my existence does not count. I have an opinion, I have a voice. I am in the room and I am worthy of respect.

Love Deeply

Throughout all my relationships there is one fact that I know to be true. I have loved deeply. I have loved with all my heart, all my soul, and my mind. I never let circumstances keep me from loving deeply. A colleague once told me that I love backwards, and I have found this to be true. Most people ease their way into a friendship. They hang out, try to get a feel for honesty or compatibility. They test the waters to before they dive in, and over time they begin to have feelings for and care about that individual, then eventually they share the emotion of love or fall in love. Not me, I dive right in. I love first. I want to be friends with everyone. I seek out a mutual interest, and I give everyone the benefit of the doubt. Then I find out who they really are, and their true character and intentions surface. Because I love backwards, I continue to get hurt. It's not necessarily a bad thing to love first, but I have had to learn to establish boundaries.

Hardships happen in relationships that allow us to lose trust. We are sometimes misunderstood and disrespected. Relationships are bound to be challenged, but when you love deeply, those challenges are that much easier to overcome. If that relationship does come to end, then you can walk away knowing that you gave your best, knowing that you loved deeply.

Pray

This is not a lecture on praying. This is not a how-to guide. This is simply me sharing my experience with you about my prayer time. I thank God every morning when I wake up for my freedom, health, and family, and yes, of course, when I have something big going on. But I will first confess that I don't pray enough.

I don't have a prayer time, prayer closet, or prayer chair, but I do recognize when the Lord stops me in my tracks and asks me to bow my head. I have a devotional calendar on my dresser, in my bathroom, and "daily word" is automatically timed on my iPhone. I do want to have a relationship with God. His love and mercy are the only reasons I am alive today. Through the loss of my son, my incarceration, my divorce, and my cancer, He never left my side. He was standing beside me when my children and grandchildren were born healthy. He was watching from afar when I opened my first business and has watched over it each day since. And when I remarried, He kicked up the wind to remind me that I had come through the storm. When I decided to write this book, He was my strength. I wanted Him to know that I was truly thankful, so I made a decision. One decision. I began to write prayer time into my calendar. Yes, I literally schedule Him in daily. It says, "Tuesday, 8:30 a.m. God." I set my alarm just as I do for any important meeting. Sometimes we have coffee. I can reschedule without condemnation or criticism when I've had a tough day. I rearrange other meetings to meet with God. I'm making great progress in my prayer life. God is keeping His word, and so am I.

To Dig Deeper, Answer The Following Question(s)

Write a paragraph explaining why you are worthy of respect.

Name one thing that you can start today to create a healthy habit.

Do you have a consistent prayer routine? What can you do to prioritize your time with God?

CHAPTER 11

FREEDOM

My freedom is something I never take for granted. It's the very first thing that I thank God for. This word has kept me on a straight and narrow path for 25 years. There is nothing more important to me than my freedom. I was in a room with over 200 people and everyone of us received a word from a stranger to talk about. My word was freedom and it literally brings me to my knees when I think about this moment in my life.

One word changed my life. One moment defined me. One decision brought me to my purpose. I challenge myself every day to live my best life so that I can inspire and empower others to live theirs. Find your word, find your freedom. You have the key to set yourself free.

Getting Through the Gate

If you ever have an opportunity to visit a military installation, you must pass a background and security clearance check to get through the gates and onto the base or post. Well, I was not aware of this the first time I went on a date with a man who is active-duty military.

My criminal offense happened over twenty years before I met this man, in another life, to another person. I avoided courthouses, jails, and applications that require a background check. There are certain exceptions for employers depending on the level and type of conviction. My offense is not to be taken lightly by any means, it was originally considered a misdemeanor offense, violated by probation and punishable as a felony. It didn't matter if I got caught for stealing a candy bar or robbing a bank. The fact remained that I had been incarcerated and I was embarrassed and ashamed about it. I feared being judged.

So, there I was at the gate with a man whose credentials met my prayer criteria, fearfully handing over my identification to a stern-faced soldier. Keep in mind I was already a very successful and established member of society.

In fact, I was earning a six-figure salary at one of the world's largest corporations and living in an upscale downtown loft on the same floor with famous people I'd never heard of. The night before my date I had attended a gala fundraiser and sat with the mayor. By the time I had realized that the soldier was inputting my information into the National Criminal Information System, it was too late to run. I had not told my date that I had a conviction. I was sick to my stomach. I was in straight panic mode and could feel the sweat beads rolling down my face. This was it, this was my biggest fear. I would be rejected and judged. As my date sat there making small talk while we waited, I tried to catch my breath and rehearse what I was going to say. I didn't go around telling everyone my life story, and I thought if he didn't understand, well, I had to let it go. Besides, it wasn't like I was going to marry the guy.

Several minutes later, the gatekeeper soldier returned with the same stern face and handed me my identification card and said, "Have a nice evening, ma'am". When I stood up, I felt exhausted. I had allowed my fear to take over my life. I don't remember any of the date, but I did eventually tell the guy my life story. And I married him.

You can bet that I have a new attitude each time I hand

over my credentials to get through the gate at the military installation, where I live with my husband. I have also earned the respect to travel freely through the gates at the Department of Corrections where I teach courses on compassion training to new recruits.

Taking Off the Shackles

I had just trudged through twenty-five years of my life, figuratively shackled to the fear of rejection and judgment. On July 19, 2018 in Fort Lauderdale, Florida, I was offered the opportunity to write a book. It has not been an easy process. I had to do what I had been avoiding for twenty-five years. I had to look back.

I admitted to myself that I still had some healing to do. I had to be honest with myself and with my family. I relived the twelve minutes of the life and loss of my son in that hospital room. I reached out to colleagues because the anxiety of being in a small space returned along with the nightmares of hearing cell blocks closing and keys clanging together. I angrily recalled the inhuman treatment I received in the hospital where my daughter was born. I felt the relief of the shackle as it released from my ankle during birth. I remember the feeling and look of compassion in the security guard's eyes, and I relived the moment my daughter was taken from me. In my mind, I returned to that cell with an empty womb, childless.

I revisited my youth and my first marriage. I was able to reminisce on good times and pull out lessons from those challenging times. I laughed thinking about all the jobs I've had, the day I challenged myself to go back school, and the students who thought I was the teacher. I rejoiced in the blessings of my true friends. I was grateful for my community finding me worthy to help raise over five thousand children in my nonprofit career. I fell in love all over again with the man God felt worthy enough to have me because he supports and believes in me. I was able to see the true glory of God in my children and grandchildren. It has not been easy, but it has been worth it. I am worth it.

I found the courage to share my story of overcoming my fears in hopes that you may find just one nugget of strength inside of you that will encourage and inspire you to make one decision. The decision to set yourself free.

YOU are the key to unshackle success.

To Dig Deeper, Answer The Following Question(s)

☐

What is your word?

What will your new attitude say about you?

What can you unshackle in your life to move forward into a life of happiness and success?

"Your Best Days are Still Ahead"

- Pastor Dennis Leonard
Heritage Christian Center
Denver CO

Pastor D.—You were my man with a pitcher of water.
There are no words to thank you for planting these words
in my spirit 20 years ago, one snowy Wednesday night service
in Denver, CO.

Rest in Peace
11/01/2018

Made in the USA
San Bernardino, CA
19 January 2019